My First ABC

Sticker Activity Book

Look for the erasers at the front of the book.
You will need them to complete some of the activities.
Next, find the sticker sheets at the back of the book.
When you are sure you have found the right sticker,
carefully peel it off and stick it down. There are also extra
stickers to use in the book or anywhere you want!

make believe ideas

Have fun exploring this sticker activity book. With your
erasers and your **stickers**, you're ready to get started!

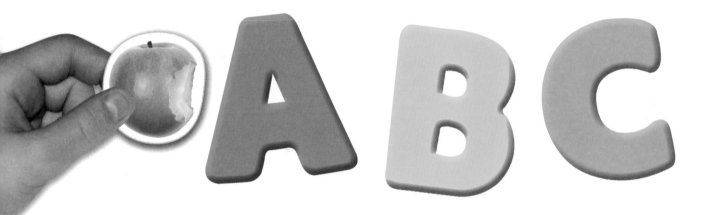

Each page focuses on a different letter of the alphabet.
Can you spot the animals and objects that begin with each letter?

D is for **drum.**

B is for **butterfly.**

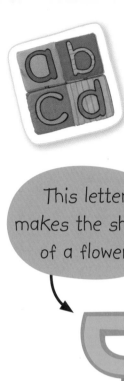

Some pages include letters hidden in other objects and shapes. You can also find letters in the things around you. How many different letters can you see?

This letter makes the shape of a flower.

This letter makes the shape of two mountains.

You can use your **erasers** to help you draw objects, trace lines, create cool designs, or for anything else you want!

Have fun!

3

Aa

Circle the fruit that is not an **apple**.

Color the pattern inside the **apple**.

Find the missing stickers to help **Alfie** complete his collection.

How many **acorns** does **Alfie** have? Write the **answer**.

Bb

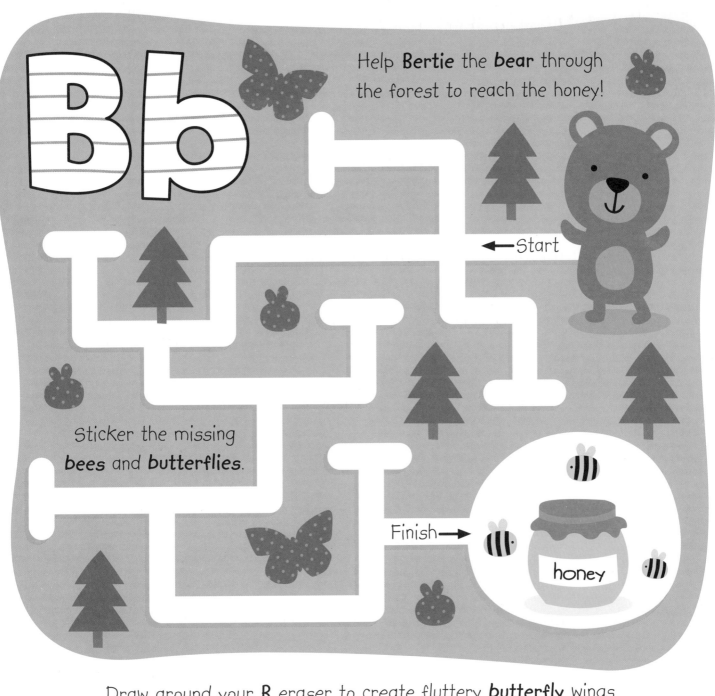

Help **Bertie** the **bear** through the forest to reach the honey!

← Start

Sticker the missing **bees** and **butterflies**.

Finish →

honey

Draw around your **B** eraser to create fluttery **butterfly** wings.

Cc

Use an eraser to trace the lines and find out which **car** is going to the **castle**.

Color the **castle**.

Color Clara the **cat**, then use stickers to **complete** the patterns.

Dd

Draw around your **A** eraser to add **details** to the **dinosaur**.

Color the **dinosaur's** spots.

Find the missing stickers, then circle the instrument beginning with **D**.

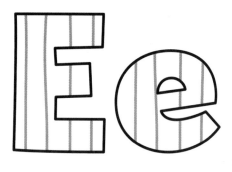

Decorate the **elephant** parade with stickers and color!

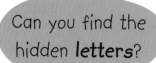

Can you find the hidden **letters**?

Ff

Create **funny faces** using color and stickers. Pay attention to the clues on the photographs!

Shade this space with a pencil, then use an eraser to rub out **fantastic fireworks**.

I have red hair.

I have green glasses.

I have a pink bow.

I have a yellow hat.

I have a blue bow tie.

Fold the page along the dashed line to **find** the **flower**.

Gg

Complete the **garden** scene with color and stickers.

How many birds can you count? Write the answer.

Color the flowers **growing** in the **garden**.

The **garden gnomes** are fishing. Use an eraser
to trace the lines and see who has caught the fish.

Find the
missing stickers.

GREEN

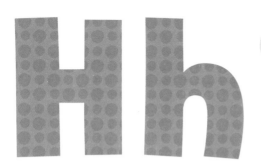

Hh

Use the grids to **help** you draw the other **half** of each picture. Finish the pictures by adding color.

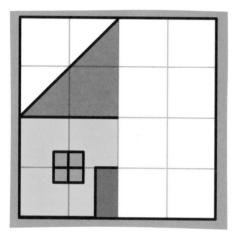
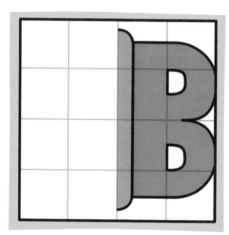
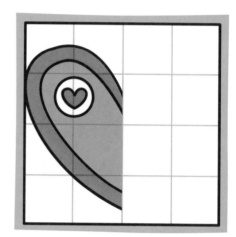

Sticker more **houses** on the **hill**. Point to the **hidden H**.

Use stickers to solve the problems.

2 + 2 =

2 − 1 =

Sticker toppings on the **ice-cream cone**.

Find stickers to complete the **ice-cream** patterns.

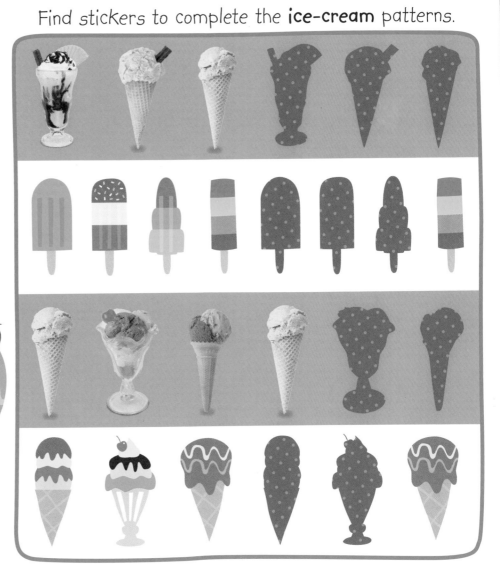

Can you circle five differences between the pictures below?

Jj

Add stickers to the **jungle** scene, then use wild colors to finish it!

How many **jaguars** can you count? Write the answer.

Kk

Find the **king** a shiny crown to wear.

Color the picture using the **key** below.

1 2 3 4 5 6

Sticker bows on the **kite's** tail.

Ll

Use the **ladders** to help **Larry** the **lion** reach the top of the **lighthouse**.

Finish

Start →

How many *seagulls* can you count? Write the answer.

Draw around your **C** eraser to create big waves in the sea.

Mm

Millie the **mouse** is camping. Look at the list below. Can you find everything in the picture?

Point to the hidden **M**.

2 **mountains** | 1 **moon** | 1 **mouse** | 2 **marshmallows** | 1 glass of **milk**

Nn

Find the missing stickers to match the **noises** to the correct animals.

How many horseshoes
can you count?
Write the answer.

Hoot!

Can you find **nine** mice?

Cluck!

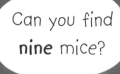

19

Oo

Find the missing stickers, then draw lines to match the **opposites**.

cold

Oscar

inside

short

hot

tall

slow

Oscar

outside

fast

20

Build a food machine with color and stickers.
Circle the food that begins with an O.

Point to the food that looks like an O.

Draw your favorite food on the plate.

Pp

Decorate the **picture** with color and stickers, then draw a **playful pet** in the frame.

My **pet's** name: ....

Sticker a ball for the **puppy**.

Sticker a kitten on the cushion.

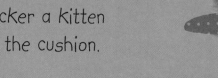

Sticker a carrot for the rabbit.

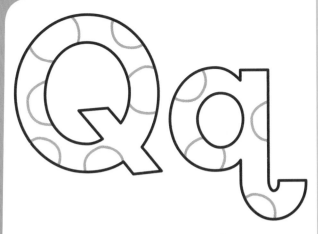

Find the missing stickers, then circle the answer to each **question** in the **quiz**.

sunglasses

hat

shoes

Which animal lives in water?

cat

guinea pig

fish

squirrel

Which animal can fly?

mouse

bird

hamster

What grows in the ground?

candy

potatoes

ice cream

cupcake

Rr

Find the missing stickers to help **Ryan** the **robot** build a **rocket**.

How many **red** gears does **Ryan** have?
Write the answer.

Draw around your erasers to add details to the **rocket**.

Decorate the scene with color and stickers.

25

S s

Help **Sarah** make a **sand castle** at the **seaside**. Use bright colors and **stickers**!

Use **stickers** to complete the **shell** patterns.

Tt

The **toys** are having a fancy **tea** party.
Finish the scene using color and stickers.

Toys

Draw around your **C** eraser to create **three** cute **teacups**.

Uu

Draw around your **C** eraser to create **umbrellas**.

Shade this storm cloud with a pencil, then **use** an eraser to rub out some raindrops.

Help Rosie the rabbit through the **underground** maze to find her rabbit friend.

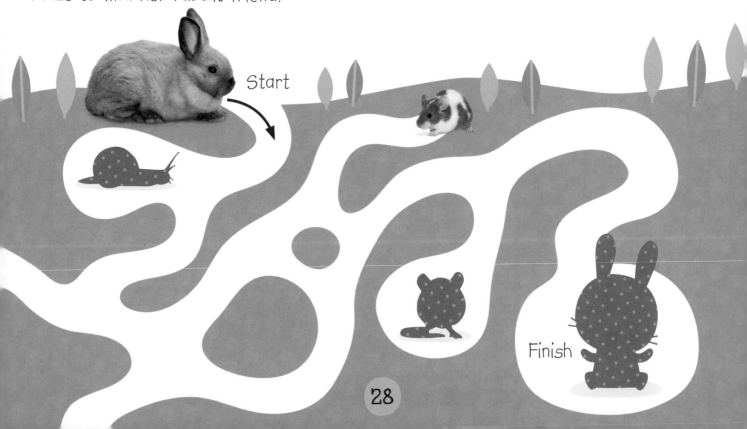

Start

Finish

28

Sticker and doodle funny faces on the **vegetables**.

Use an eraser to trace the lines and find out who reaches the **van**.

Victor

Veronica

Vickie

X x

X marks the spot! Use color and stickers to complete the treasure map, then draw a path through the ocean to help the ship reach the X.

Start

Find a pirate hat for me to wear.

Sticker and color to fill the
page with **yellow** things.

Can **you** reach
the star in the middle
of the **yo-yo** maze?

Start

Z z

Draw stripes on the **zebras**, then use stickers to complete the **zoo**.

penguins

giraffe

lions

elephant

Use color and stickers to fill the frames.

Create a pretty flower garden with stickers and color.

Point to the hidden **letters**.

Add color to complete the patterns.

Use color and stickers to create an underwater scene.
Draw around your erasers to finish the fish.

A

B C

Point to the hidden **letters**.

Draw around your **A** eraser to add a roof to the castle.

How many starfish can you count? Write the answer.

Decorate the **alphabet** superhero with stickers and color.

Point to the hidden **letters**.

Use stickers and doodles to fill
this page with **letter** monsters.

Finish the clothesline using color and stickers.

Point to the hidden **letters**.

Shade this top with a pencil, then use an eraser to rub out a design.

How many socks are on the clothesline? Write the answer.

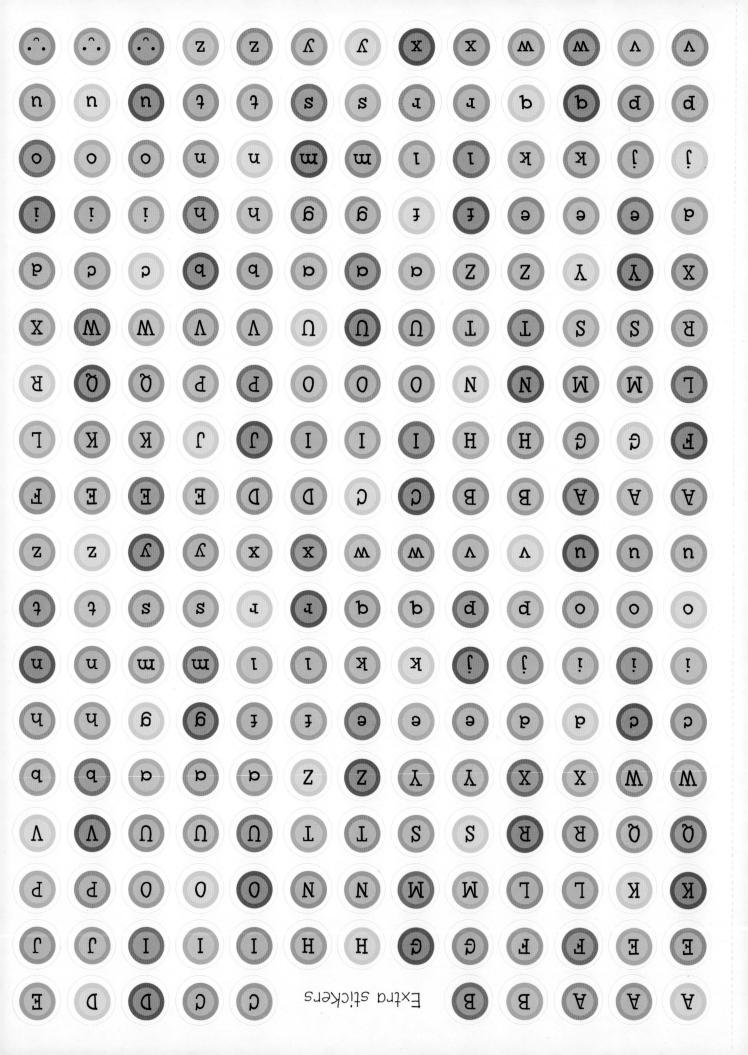

Extra stickers

Page 40

Pages 36-39

Pages 34-35

Page 33 continued

Pages 32-33

Pages 28-29

Pages 30-31

Pages 26-27

Pages 22-25

Pages 20-21

Cock-a-doodle-doo!

Neigh!

Oink!

Baa!

Pages 16-19

Pages 14-15

Pages 12-13

Pages 8-11

Pages 6-7

Pages 4-5